CW00661587

BETTER THAN
OR EQUAL TO?

Also available in the Pioneer *Perspectives* series:

Prophecy in the Church	Martin Scott
Radical Evangelism	Pete Gilbert
Relationships—Jesus Style	Stuart Lindsell
The Role and Ministry of Women	Martin Scott
The Worshipping Church	Noel Richards

For further information on the Pioneer *Perspectives* series and Pioneer, please write to:

P.O. Box 79c, Esher, Surrey, KT10 9LP

BETTER THAN OR EQUAL TO?

A Look at Singleness

Linda Harding

WORD PUBLISHING

Word (UK) Ltd
Milton Keynes, England

WORD AUSTRALIA
Kilsyth, Victoria, Australia

WORD COMMUNICATIONS LTD
Vancouver, B.C., Canada

STRUIK CHRISTIAN BOOKS (PTY) LTD
Maitland, South Africa

CHRISTIAN MARKETING NEW ZEALAND LTD
Havelock North, New Zealand

JENSCO LTD
Hong Kong

JOINT DISTRIBUTORS SINGAPORE –
ALBY COMMERCIAL ENTERPRISES PTE LTD
and
CAMPUS CRUSADE

SALVATION BOOK CENTRE
Malaysia

BETTER THAN OR EQUAL TO?

© Pioneer 1993.

Published by Word (UK) Ltd. / Pioneer 1993.

All rights reserved. No part of this publication may be reproduced or transmitted in any form or by any means, electronic or mechanical, including photocopying, recording, or any information storage or retrieval system, without permission in writing from the publisher.

ISBN 0-85009-729-0   (Australia ISBN 1-86258-248-3)

Unless otherwise indicated, Scripture quotations are from the HOLY BIBLE, NEW INTERNATIONAL VERSION (NIV). Copyright © 1973, 1978, 1984 by International Bible Society.
Other quotations are from the New English Bible, © 1961, 1970 by the Delegates of the Oxford University Press and the Syndics of the Cambridge University Press; the Revised Standard Version, © 1971 by Division of Christian Education of the National Council of Churches of Christ in the United States of America.

Front cover illustration: *Sunflowers*, Vincent van Gogh, courtesy of Bridgeman Art Library.

Printed in England by Clays Ltd, St Ives plc

93 94 95 96 / 10 9 8 7 6 5 4 3 2 1

FOREWORD

Pioneer *Perspectives* are perhaps more than their title suggests!

They are carefully researched presentations of material, on important issues, appealing to thinking churches, creative leaders and responsible Christians.

Each *Perspective* pioneers in as much as it is at the cutting edge of biblical and theological issues. Each will continue to pioneer with new ideas, concepts and data drawn from Scripture, history and a contemporary understanding of both.

They are perspectives in as much as they aim to be an important contribution to the ongoing debate on issues such as women in ministry and leadership; prophets and prophecy in the church; biblical models of evangelism; integrating and discipling new believers; growing and building local churches and further perspectives on Christ's second coming.

Importantly, these studies use a journal style of presentation, and are written by people who are currently working out the implications of the issues they are writing about, in local churches. This is vital if we are to escape the dangerous fantasy of abstract theology without practical experience. They are not written to contribute to the paralysis of analysis—rather to feed, strengthen, nurture and inform so that we can be equipped to get God's will done, by networking the nations with the gospel using all the resources that are available to us.

God's Word is always an event. How much we thank Him that He has left us an orderly account of what He wants us to believe, how He wants us to live, and what He wants us to do in order to bring heaven to the earth. As we embrace a better understanding of

Scripture, rooted in local church, national and
international mission, we shall become a part of the
great eschatological purpose of bringing back the
King—not for a church defeated, cowering and retiring
but for one which, despite colossal odds, pressures and
persecutions, is faithful to her Lord and His Word. To
do that we must 'search the Scriptures' to see if many of
these 'new things' are true. I commend these
Perspectives to you as they are published on a regular
basis throughout these coming years.

Gerald Coates
Director Pioneer Trust/Team Leader

Pioneer consists of a team and network of churches, committed to dynamic and effective biblical Christianity.

The national team act as advisers and consultants to churches, which in many cases develop into a partnership with the Pioneer team. These are the churches keen to identify with the theology, philosophy, ethos and purpose of Pioneer. The team have a vigorous youth ministry, church-planting strategy and evangelistic emphasis.

Training courses include Equipped to Lead, Emerging Leaders and the highly successful TIE teams (Training In Evangelism).

Pioneer have also been instrumental in initiating and funding March for Jesus (with Ichthus/YWAM); Jubilee Campaign (for the suffering church worldwide); and ACET (Aids Care Education Training).

ACKNOWLEDGEMENTS

Firstly this book is a tribute to Paul and Margaret, Nicola, Jennie and Michael, who opened their lives and their home to me in a way that enabled me to be a whole person. Without them the contents of this book would not have been born.

I would like to express my thanks to my friends in Pioneer People and other Pioneer churches who, having invited me to share my own experiences and perspectives of singleness, encouraged me to believe that I had something to write about; to Stuart for his support in releasing my time to write the book; to Martin, Paul, Pat, Chris and Sal for their helpful comments, and also to Lyn, Kate and Judy.

Most of all to my closest friend, Val, with whom I am discovering some of the dimension of the companionship between David and Jonathan. Thank you for your understanding and patience through the process of putting these words into print.

Linda Harding
August 1992

CONTENTS

INTRODUCTION

Why a Pioneer *Perspective* on singleness?

Singles are a significant people group, forming approximately one-third of the adult population, and, more than at any other time in history, the numbers are increasing. Singleness as a topic immediately leads to a list of questions:

- What does the Bible say about singleness?
- Is marriage God's best and therefore are single people the victims of statistics and a life that is second-best in God's purpose?
- If we see marriage as the only answer to the statement 'it is not good that man should be alone', where does that leave hundreds of men and woman who for many reasons are on their own?
- What is God's plan and does it relate to singleness?
- Is the calling of celibacy only for priests and nuns?
- Is the gospel good news to single people? Is it possible to live a fulfilled life as a single in a couple-orientated society?
- Is there a place for a 'one' person in a church that is illustrated as 'family'?
- In a sex-mad culture, are biblical standards of morality unrealistic and out of date?
- Is the church able to reach out with an attractive and relevant message to single men and women?

- What is the message and model we are giving our children?
- What is the church's response to the increasing number of parents seeking to bring up children on their own?
- What about those whose partner has died?
- And what of the many who have been damaged by divorce, desertion or separation?

The presence of single people in increasing numbers presents a huge challenge to the church in the '90s. Every church has, or will have, single people of many different backgrounds and experiences. Many who are married now may one day be single again. Parents need to face the challenge in relation to their children. In short, the church's response to singleness is relevant for all of us to consider.

Many books have been written for single people about the problems of singleness. This book seeks to take a positive approach. It addresses a challenge to the church to be leading the way, to be a pacesetter, responding to the changing demography and prepared for increasing numbers of single adults. It is intended therefore to be relevant for the whole church, to equip us to integrate all people groups and to increase our understanding of the special needs of each distinctive 'group' in order to offer effective pastoral care. To be single in the '90s requires faith and to live a celibate lifestyle requires an understanding of God's calling and courage to walk in it. In this decade the church has the opportunity to be God's provision of a prophetic community, with a radical and challenging message.

The aim of this Pioneer *Perspective* is:

- To increase understanding of a biblical perspective on singleness and to see the place of singleness in the purposes of God.
- To raise awareness of attitudes and issues

relating to singleness, of the needs and potential of single people.
- To envision and equip the church to respond creatively and practically to this significant people group, seeing it as an opportunity, not a problem.

PART ONE

CHAPTER 1

SINGLES: WHO ARE THEY?

What does single mean? Answers in word association exercises include one, alone, unwanted, rejection, free, young, frustration, frigid, even 'cream'! The *Oxford Dictionary* definition is 'one only, not double, one by itself, unmarried, lonely, unaided'.

Historically, 'single' has described those who have never married, or been in a sexual relationship. The increase in sexual promiscuity, cohabitation, breakdown of marriage and open homosexuality has altered the concept of singleness. Singles are a diverse group and the label of 'singles' can really only be used descriptively. For the purpose of this *Perspective* it includes those who are:

- single, never married, with no sexual experience;
- single, with a history of cohabiting or other sexual relationships;
- single, never married, with a child or children;
- single but previously married, now separated, deserted, divorced or widowed; with or without children.

Some single people live alone, others with a family; single people may live with other singles, with parents or children. Some would consider themselves single by circumstances while others remain single by choice or as part of their calling. Some are single because they do not feel able to be married at present due to HIV or AIDS, sexual abuse or homosexual orientation.

Within the above 'groupings' each individual may be at different stages in their perception of singleness. Some are fully content to be single, others are enjoying the single life, but desiring marriage. Many are single and wishing to be married at any cost. These are those who often value marriage more than who they marry.

Each single person is an individual, with different attitudes to singleness, and different experiences. Some will have had pleasant experiences of relationships, and many will have been hurt. Some may see themselves remaining single in the short term, others for the foreseeable future. For some singleness is a challenge, for others a crisis.

Whatever their current situation, most single men and women will share a common understanding of the status of marriage and singleness, and of the pressures of coping with certain issues. These relate to identity, loneliness, responsibilities at home and work, family and children and a sense of loss.

The following statistics give some idea of the significance of this people group in the UK:

- One in four households are single-person households.
- One in five families are lone-parent families.
- One in three births were to unmarried women in 1990.
- The divorce rate in the UK has doubled in the last twenty years, with one in three first marriages ending in divorce, and one in two where the couple are younger than twenty-one.
- The rate of remarriage is increasing, with 72% of men and 57% of women divorced between 1977 and 1980 remarrying within five years. Current trends indicate that one in two of these marriages end in another divorce.

- One in three of the adult population are single, that is over eleven million adults in Britain, of whom one million are single parents.*

These figures are estimated to rise so *the single population is growing!*

---

* Office of Population Census and Surveys, 'Population Trends April 1991' (HMSO)
Relate, 'Family Policy Briefing' (1990)

CHAPTER 2

ATTITUDES TO SINGLENESS

This chapter looks at attitudes to singleness, first in society generally, and then in the church through its history.

Society

In our couple-orientated society, partnership is the norm. Being part of a couple is acceptable and a sign of success in a world where the basic unit is two. Marriage is seen as a status symbol. Having a partner increases a person's perceived worth or value. Marriage or co-habitation are goals, because society perceives them as providing a high level of fulfilment. Heterosexual partnership is seen as a sign of adult maturity: single men are often perceived by society as irresponsible or immature, unwilling to take on responsibility or commit themselves. It is interesting to note that almost all successful men (in business and in the church) are married—a man may think he needs a wife and family in order to succeed.

Single women are often seen as independent and headstrong, or aggressive, a situation frequently brought about in order to survive battles with the bank manager, the garage or the plumber! Alternatively the picture may be that of a weak and vulnerable woman with no initiative. To be single after the age of thirty for a woman is seen as definitely odd.

Because people perceive the value and status of

the single life as low, many single people live with the belief that something is wrong with them. Our society implies the silent message that singles are abnormal, unacceptable and carry a sense of failure.

The hierarchy as perceived by society goes something like this:

- Cohabitation
- Marriage
- Divorced
- Single, never married.

(This may be different if a single person has children.) How many times do single people hear statements such as 'I cannot understand why you have never married?' as though one deserves marriage if intelligent, good-looking or an interesting person! Finding a marriage partner is seen as a reward (often for good looks). Failure to marry therefore, by implication, can be felt to be a punishment for the inability to 'earn' a partner.

Most of us are brought up with an expectation from our parents that we will get married. The question asked of most young adults in their twenties or thirties concerns *when* you are getting married rather than *if* you will marry. The commonest questions usually contain a negative, for example: 'Why *aren't* you married?' and are insensitive and inappropriate. The questions highlight the inequality of status since married people are never asked the question 'Why are you married' or 'Why are you not single?'

As one gets older there is a silent assumption that one has been married or in a cohabiting relationship. So the question then changes to 'Have you been married?' It appears almost more acceptable to have been married than never to have married.

Many women struggle with the fact that they have never been asked to marry, and men can battle with having been rejected, so jokes or comments about singleness can cause pressure for single people. So can unhelpful labels such as 'feminist', 'go-getter', or 'set-in-his-ways bachelor'. *The Oxford Dictionary* defines 'spinster' as 'woman thought unlikely to marry'. Words such as 'spinster', 'bachelor', 'celibate', 'virgin', conjure up negative images in most people's minds. 'Spinster' has connotations of frustration and frigidity. Some psychologists speak of bachelors and spinsters as emotionally incomplete. Freud describes virgins as disturbed and unbalanced. Society links personal worth to sexual achievement. The popular image of a single woman is that of timid spinster or domineering career woman, and of a single man that of playboy, with its association of irresponsibility.

Singleness can evoke feelings of pity or, at times, a patronising attitude towards the 'misfits' in society. Society cannot handle the fact that a single person can be content and therefore commonly delivers messages of disbelief, fear or threat. Single people can also be the target of suspicion, especially if developing committed friendships with the same sex. Two men or two women living together, or taking holidays together, are assumed to be in a practising homosexual or lesbian relationship. A single person living with a married couple or family is considered to be a bit eccentric.

Most parents expect their children to marry, and put pressure—spoken or unspoken—on their adult sons and daughters. Parents themselves can receive messages of suspicion or failure from their peers if their adult offspring remain unmarried.

As a result of these pressures by society, many single people rush into marriage, afraid of being 'left on the shelf' with all the stigma that carries, of disappointing their parents, or of facing life without companionship, children and sexual fulfilment.

This, then, is our society's vision of singleness and therefore also of marriage. It becomes even more pronounced in many 'two-thirds world' cultures where parents arrange marriages, and where singleness is totally unacceptable, and much misunderstood.

Church

I wonder if attitudes in the church are at times reflective of society. *What is the church's vision of and for single people?*

The church portrayed as family may present an unhelpful image to those grappling with not being within a family unit, and single people often feel marginalised. Two or three hundred years ago the calling of singleness to serve God was emphasised in the church and marriage was downgraded. In this century even the Christian subculture celebraïes marriage to the exclusion of singleness and many single people feel undervalued in church.

It is interesting that many overseas mission organisations rely heavily on single women. A hundred or more years ago single missionaries often took the gospel overseas to unreached nations. A survey of 40 major missionary societies conducted by the Evangelical Alliance in 1984 found that 33% of the workers overseas in the 35–44 age group were single women. Yet the church can fail to acknowledge these pioneering people, who sacrificed marriage and family and home for the Kingdom. Single missionaries have become the butt of jokes, seen as unattractive and somewhat eccentric, labelled as 'escaping the rigours of the world'. There may be some truth in this picture but many of these missionaries have in fact embraced Jesus' teaching on renouncing marriage for the sake of the Kingdom. We need to consider our attitude to single missionaries, usually women, returning from the mission field. The church needs to find creative ways to respond to these pioneers, to help them to find a place of value and honour in the local church.

Much Christian writing and teaching which relates to marriage and the importance of family, though biblical, can reinforce the feeling that marriage is God's best. The shadow of that teaching produces a subtle message—singleness is second-best. This negative view of singleness is clearly unbiblical. The church has presented marriage as fulfilling and therefore singleness, by default, as unfulfilling. Marriage is seen as a focal point and so people are perceived as 'waiting to get married', 'not yet married' or 'having been married'.

The same Christians who would say that everyone is complete in Christ are often those who try to matchmake, or see single people as a problem, thus contradicting their own theology. Marriage is subtly modelled as a goal which will provide the answer to loneliness and questions of identity and which will satisfy the need for success. Whilst marriage may be part of an answer, it is a myth to present marriage as *the* answer to all our needs for self-worth, security and significance. The church needs to be careful that it is not conforming to the world's message.

In the church, a single man of thirty may be perceived as *going for God* while a single woman of the same age carries a feeling of *not having made it*. The church adds to the pressure by teaching the importance of being 'equally yoked with believers'. Because most churches have a surplus of women over men, statistically many Christian women face the reality of a single lifestyle. This appears to result from circumstances rather than choice. It is important that the church encourages each individual in these situations to take responsibility for their choices, so that they will not turn round and blame the church when they are still single ten years later.

The promise that '[God] will give you the desires of your heart' (Ps. 37:4), can be very damaging if given glibly and without the context of 'Delight yourself in the Lord'. Many single people live with unfulfilled desires in respect of marriage, naively believing that coming to Christ would mean finding a Christian husband or wife. Some conclude that they have failed if the promise does not become a reality, others blame God for not answering their prayer.

If personal experience is boxed into stereotypes with no real understanding, the relationships between married and single people in the church can be marred. Singles may envy marrieds, married people may envy singles, view them with suspicion or see divorced people as a threat. Many married people who have not consciously experienced singleness cannot imagine how they would cope with being single, so they assume responsibility for finding a marriage partner for their single friends. They can expend energy praying to this end because they believe that marriage is best, and that somehow usefulness in the church is increased with a marriage partner. The church can be more committed to matchmake for single people than help them to find God's best for their life, which may not include a marriage partner.

People find it impossible to believe that an individual could be satisfied and fulfilled as a single person. A further pressure in the church can result from the belief that single people have lots of time, and therefore they are free to serve married people in a variety of practical ways. Another perception is that single people have lots of money. Single people *may* have more time and money but they also have the freedom to choose how to use them. Married people have sacrificed that freedom and need to guard against making judgements.

God created marriage to be a permanent union, and conflict and breakdown in marriage were never His intention. The church, by teaching that divorce is the result of sinful nature, can add condemnation to divorced people who, already weighed down with shame and failure, can feel unaccepted in the family of God.

It is important to be careful of stereotyping the roles, attitudes, responses and problems of single people. *Single people are not a special breed—they are first and foremost people who happen to be single today.*

CHAPTER 3

BIBLICAL PERSPECTIVE

Before looking specifically at biblical references to singleness, it is worth highlighting the overall message of God's nature. He cares for each individual, whoever they are, whatever their circumstances. Jesus offers freedom and hope especially to marginalised people, to orphans, to the fatherless and to widows.

There is very little in the Bible on singleness because hardly anyone remained unmarried in Bible times and therefore singleness was not a topic of high cultural relevance. However, what is recorded is significant and important, but has caused some confusion historically because of apparent contradictions.

But what was God's plan?

The creation order shows that God's image included male and female. God made men and women to be in relationship and together reflect His image. But is this relationship exclusively marriage?

God's plan was for companionship and procreation, and marriage was planned by God to give the first man and woman a permanent and complete union. But sin came and spoiled God's original plan, and thereafter sin taints all our relationships, both with God and with each other, marriage included. However when Jesus came to reconcile us to God, He also came to show that in the relationship with God made possible through Him, there is completeness. It has been said that in Adam we see the perfection of marriage, and in Jesus, the second Adam, we see the perfection of singleness. Jesus came to show a new way redeeming both marriage and singleness so that *both* can show God's glory to a fallen world.

Old Testament

Marriage was so much the norm in the Jewish culture that there is no Hebrew word for bachelor. It was the parental duty to find a marriage partner, to the extent that a slave was used as a last resort. Marriage was only delayed after the age of twenty to study the law, as a vocation, as a prophetic statement or to be a eunuch.

However, alongside God's plan in relation to marriage, and the cultural norm of the day, God chose some significant single men and women to serve Him in strategic ways to fulfil His purposes.

Jeremiah was told by God not to marry and his life was a prophetic statement (Jer. 16:1–15). Another major prophet, Ezekiel, was widowed (Ezek 24:15–19) and Daniel was appointed a palace eunuch (Dan. 1:3–6).

In the book of Hosea broken marriages are a sign of fallenness and God's judgement on a nation. Similarly God's blessing on a nation is sometimes seen in the restoration of the gifts of marriage and singleness as God intended them.

New Testament

Three significant people, who play an integral part in the process of God becoming man, are all single. Mary, as a single woman and a virgin, consented to bear God's Son. John the Baptist heralded the coming of Jesus, and later baptised Him. Anna, widowed after seven years of marriage, devoted herself to serve God in praying faithfully right up to the age of eighty-four.

At the centre of our faith is a God who chose to make Himself known, contrary to the prevailing culture, as a single person, fully man, tempted in every point as we are, yet able to live a fulfilled life. Jesus was certainly not a model of half a person. How would He have rated today, when success is associated with marriage?

Jesus was free to care, to form deep and satisfying relationships, to show emotion, to give Himself to others. Jesus relaxed in the home of His friends Mary, Martha and Lazarus who, as far as we know, were single people. Jesus' life was characterised by self-giving, but He also knew how to receive from His friends and to receive the outward expression of affection too. Jesus related to both men and women with purity and integrity. In each encounter with women He communicated their worth and value, He accepted and welcomed their love. He was not afraid of touch—see the story of the prostitute who wiped His feet with her hair, kissed them and poured perfume on them (Luke 7:38). Jesus' perfect example of a single life is a great encouragement for single men and women.

Both Jesus and the early church gave a special place to widows. The persistent widow in the parable in Luke 18 would not give up believing, and the generous widow in Luke 21 gave all she had to Jesus. Why did the Gospel writers record these stories of widows? Perhaps Jesus wanted to place particular emphasis on the value of a single woman in His culture. There are several other examples of single men and women in the early church in addition to Jesus—Paul, for example, and Philip's four daughters who prophesied (Acts 21:8–9).

The New Testament model is of compatibility—marriage and singleness as part of God's plan. The age to come is pictured in both: with marriage as the relationship between the church and Jesus (Eph. 5:23–32) and singleness illustrating that there will be no marriage in heaven, for Jesus taught that marriage is only for this life (Matt. 22:30).

(i) Matthew 19:3–12
This teaching is only recorded in Matthew's Gospel,

and the context is immediately after Jesus addresses questions on marriage and divorce. Jesus affirmed God's original plan of marriage but denied the absolute status, and did not promote it as the norm for everyone. Jesus showed understanding of, and supported, both single and married states. He taught that singleness is a God-given alternative to marriage for some, but not all.

When Jesus upheld the ideal of unbreakable marriage, the disciples suggested that in view of this demanding commitment and the difficulties in marriage, perhaps it was better not to marry. Jesus replied, 'Not everyone can accept this word, but only those to whom it has been given'(v.11). This suggests that Jesus is highlighting the cost of marriage and affirming marriage as a calling for those who are able to receive it. But following this, He says that celibacy is given to some and commends the unmarried state to those whose call demands it. Jesus upholds the high calling of giving up marriage for the sake of the Kingdom—that people moved by the crisis and challenge of proclaiming the Kingdom might forego the opportunity to marry. He explains different reasons for being single. There are natural reasons, as some are born with physical disability leaving them impotent*, others are made physically impotent by men (not uncommon in the culture) and 'others have renounced marriage because of the kingdom of heaven' (v.12—literally 'made themselves eunuchs') i.e. *some have chosen to be single in order to give time and energy to serve God.* Celibacy was unusual in the Jewish society, and generally linked to physical incapacity (whether natural or man-inflicted).

It would appear that Jesus here is broadening the reasons for celibacy beyond that of physical incapacity or natural circumstances. He is describing a state of *voluntary celibacy,* in which people have abstained from

---

* Jesus is explaining here that impotence may be a reason to remain single, but He is not stating that impotence means you cannot marry.

marriage in order to devote themselves more wholeheartedly to serve the Kingdom. He infers that those who marry and have a family have special responsibilities which demand attention and time and therefore limit their availability. However, Jesus made it clear again that only some could 'accept' this teaching and encourages those that can to do so.

(ii) 1 Corinthians 7

Paul builds on the foundation of Jesus' teaching. His teaching on celibacy is also set in the context of teaching on marriage. The passage in 1 Corinthians 7 is sometimes quoted to support a higher calling of singleness, or to suggest that Paul was anti-marriage. However, in Ephesians 5 Paul speaks of the mystery of marriage, illustrating the union of Christ and His church, honouring Christian marriage as God-appointed.

Paul clearly believed in and promoted both marriage and singleness as valid alternatives, with neither state being superior or inferior. He is not downgrading marriage, but raising the status of singleness. Paul affirms the value of singleness and the celibate lifestyle and, despite his personal preference for singleness, he is also very clear in upholding the sanctity of marriage. Paul repeats the earlier teaching of Jesus, explaining that the single life is a gift from God which was preferable for himself, but outlining the difficulties which ensue if those who have not received the gift of celibacy try to live a single life. Paul is not promoting singleness for its own sake. He underlines that both marriage and singleness are gifts, 'Each man has his own gift from God; one has this gift, another has that' (1 Cor. 7:7). Note the equal status in this phrase.

In order to interpret the relevance of these passages it is important to understand the context into which Paul was writing. Corinth was a place with much sexual immorality. The Corinthian church faced questions concerning the viability of living with your sexuality if unmarried, and of maintaining Christian marriage within a pagan society. In the sexually charged environment at Corinth, some saw liberty as meaning sexual freedom. In response to concerns and problems in this situation Paul affirms the value of sex within marriage, and advises marriage as a safeguard in a society full of temptation. He also highlights the cost of marriage and the difficulties of putting Christ first.

To address the environment of permissiveness and unfaithfulness in Corinth, and situation ethics in the church, Paul recognises the God-appointed context of marriage for expression of the sexual drive. But he urges people to consider the single life seriously, directing their energies to serve God. He was not making a rule, but was looking realistically at marriage and singleness. He questioned the inevitability of marriage and presented singleness as a valuable, positive and acceptable option in the situation.

There is an eschatological urgency which underpins Paul's passion for celibacy, as a lifestyle with greater freedom to serve the Lord and fulfil the task of preaching the gospel to all the world. His preference for celibacy, and his desire that others should consider following his example, is written within the expectation that the present age would be consummated within their lifetime. It is also linked to the crisis of the situation of sexual permissiveness and unfaithfulness in Corinth, which must challenge us with the relevance of Paul's words in the 1990s.

Jesus and Paul speak of singleness as a gift from God for those who can accept it: it is not earned and not given to everyone. James teaches that all God's gifts are good (James 1:17) and Paul clearly refers to singleness as a good thing. We may perceive celibacy as unnatural, but so is much of Jesus' teaching, e.g. turn the other cheek, love your enemies, etc. The gift of celibacy can be seen as an unwanted gift, because our society associates singleness with failure or even punishment. What a contrast to a gift from God!

In 1 Corinthians 7:7 Paul talks about celibacy as a *charisma* (gift)—which means a specific form of grace supernaturally given to someone in order to work out God's sovereign purpose in their life. The gift of celibacy enabled Paul to fulfil the demands and cope with the pressures of God's call on his life. When the calling to serve God includes singleness, the gift of celibacy is given to those who are able to receive it for a season or perhaps for always. The focus here is on the positive gain of opportunities to love and to serve, rather than the 'giving up' of marriage and sex. Celibacy can be defined as 'abstinence from marriage'. Its value consists not in avoiding the responsibilities and cares of marriage, but in the freedom it brings to fulfil one's desire to devote time and energy to serve God.

Paul and Jesus therefore both present an option of voluntary singleness, undertaken in order to live life in undivided devotion to God. In these passages we catch a glimpse of singleness in the light of eternal values, and see the opportunities for single people to serve God.

> An unmarried man is concerned about the Lord's affairs—how he can please the Lord. But a married man is concerned about the affairs of this world—how he can please his wife—and his interests are divided. An unmarried woman . . . is concerned about the Lord's affairs: her aim is to be devoted to the Lord in both body and spirit. But a married woman is concerned about the affairs of this world—how she can please her husband (1 Cor. 7:33–34).

Is the gift of celibacy only for those who have voluntarily 'renounced marriage because of the kingdom', or is it also available to those who by choice or circumstance grow into a realisation of being single? The key lies with the willingness to receive the gift. Whether by conscious decision, i.e. 'voluntary singleness' as part of God's calling, or by a gradual realisation and acceptance of

God's will, the gift of celibacy is available. The *Oxford Dictionary* definition of a celibate is 'one resolved not to marry'. There are many Christian men and women who, recognising that real union includes spiritual oneness, have limited their choice of marriage partner. By making this decision they could be described as having resolved not to marry or 'made themselves eunuchs [incapable of marriage] for the sake of the kingdom' (Matt. 19:12 RSV).

Receiving the gift of celibacy does not require a stunting of love—it demands the sacrifice of sexual intimacy and natural parenthood, not of the ability to love deeply and to express affection. Celibacy should not be seen as a virtue, but as part, just as marriage is part, of our calling to love. Each has its sacrifices and each requires acceptance of the opportunities and the responsibilities as well as the limitations. In each the redemptive power of God can be shown. God has called us to one of these states—for *today*. The key is to walk in it. This is Paul's exhortation in 1 Corinthians 7:17: 'Each one should retain the place in life that the Lord assigned to him, and to which God has called him.'

Celibacy has been associated historically with monastic orders. Thomas Aquinas wrote that celibacy outside community is impossible—in monastic communities, men and women who had taken vows of celibacy could be closeted away from pressures and temptations. Jesus and Paul, however, did not live in a monastic community. God's redeemed community of the church should be an environment in which men and women who are seeking to live according to biblical standards of morality can be supported.

Conclusion

In summary, a biblical theology of singleness differs radically from society's view. The Christian stands out from the culture of his time by seeing the unmarried state as good.

- Marriage and singleness are gifts of grace.
- Neither lifestyle is superior or inferior.
- Both require sacrifice, and both have blessings.
- God wants both married and single people to honour Him.

CHAPTER 4

SINGLENESS : CIRCUMSTANCES OR CHOICE?

Everyone today is searching for fulfilment, i.e. *life lived to the full*. The question facing most single people is whether it is really possible to be fulfilled, since upbringing and society condition us to feel that the greatest fulfilment is found in marriage. This is undoubtedly true for many married people, but does that leave the single person to face a life of unfulfilment?

Jesus lived a fulfilled life—He was tempted to find physical fulfilment, but He resisted the temptations and lived according to His Father's will. Real fulfilment is about embracing God's plan and promises for our lives, just as Jesus did, loving God more than anything else and facing the heart-searching question of what is more important: to know God or to be married. Putting God first in our lives involves the sacrifice of surrendering to God the right to be married and the right to have children. Seeking first the Kingdom of God means submitting all our desires to Him, so that we can say with Paul, 'For to me, to live is Christ and to die is gain' (Phil. 1:21). Jesus had to suffer to fulfil God's purposes for His life. Embracing singleness, including its sacrifices, as God's present will for our lives is the only path to fulfilment. Paul writes, 'Offer your bodies [with your mind and will] as living sacrifices, holy and pleasing to God . . . Then you will be able to test and approve what God's will is—his good, pleasing [acceptable] and perfect will'(Rom. 12:1–2). Paul's teaching encourages us to be free to appreciate our present gift and to enjoy life to the full.

Fulfilment is often perceived as all needs being met. Being single can raise feelings of being unfulfilled, which is why many single people throw their lives into a career or a hobby or activity, to meet their physical and mental needs. But our primary needs as human beings for identity, security and purpose are met in God: knowing Him, knowing ourselves, and knowing His purpose. As we stay close to Jesus, and know Him as a friend, a Father, a helper, we will recognise that there are no limits to His love and care.

Intimacy in our relationship with God is an essential foundation—the key to living a single life to the full is to know that we are in Christ and He in us: 'union' with God. This is worked out at a practical level primarily through giving ourselves to others in friendship, and through involvement in church, work and home, all of which serve to add to the richness of life. Then we discover there is little room for loneliness or frustration.

A person's view of singleness will reflect their own experience or conditioning from their upbringing, although many who marry young hardly experience being single. It is challenging to see if our attitude to singleness is shaped by a secular view or by a Kingdom perspective. This is where developing an understanding of singleness from a biblical perspective can help us to find a vision for the single life in the purposes of God.

Marriage can be thought of as *the* answer to problems of singleness. In fact both singleness and marriage can be seen as absolutes. If I admit to enjoying being single then I am perceived as not desiring marriage or even as being 'anti-marriage', or, as a woman, an ardent feminist. It is possible to find satisfaction in the single life and still desire marriage— to learn with Paul the reality of being 'content whatever the circumstances' (Phil. 4:11). However, many single people find the desire for marriage becomes all-consuming, affecting every area of their life, particularly relationships. It is difficult to enjoy singleness if all one's energies are expended on trying to find a marriage partner. Many single people want to know how to *give up* the single life rather than how to live it. Despite the statistics, single life is still seen as abnormal and so being unmarried often leads to feelings of anger or bitterness. Many in the church who experience marital difficulties have been those whose feelings have led them to rush into marriage to escape being single.

Singleness is generally not a planned state but the result of natural circumstances in which no proposal of marriage is given or received, often for sociological reasons, although there may be physical or psychological disability. Most older single people have no desire to be single—they would prefer to be married and consequently feel frustrated and resentful. It is helpful for single people to realise that these feelings can be experienced in marriage too!

People's perception of their singleness varies at different ages, and some will resist facing the fact. Being single at the age of 25, 35, 45 or 55 are all very different experiences. Singleness for some can be an embarrassing or delicate subject; for others it is a big unknown.

'How do I know if celibacy is God's will for me?' is the question most frequently asked by Christian single men and women. Paul talks about living the life 'to which God has called him' (1 Cor. 7:17). We need to accept God's will for our life for the present and see that we have a gift—that of being single or married. God's plans for my life are good and pleasing. I am not 'on the shelf' but I am 'in the plan'. God promises to give me the desires of my heart if I delight in Him. The question most single people have to face is: 'What are the desires of my heart: to be married or to know God?'

Our ultimate calling and purpose as Christians is to seek God and do His will. We may desire marriage but can waste time in bitterness and self-pity if we focus on marriage so much that we fail to enjoy God's gift for today. Adjusting our sights may be difficult, but God's grace is there for us. For every Christian, single or married, the secret of contentment lies in learning to accept his or her current state—in embracing God's will for the present, rather than enduring it. Yet it is easy to see singleness as a mistake or an accident and live accordingly. Knowing God can transform singleness into a privilege as we prove He is faithful and can meet every need. The key is in accepting singleness as a gift for today. We can still recognise and acknowledge our longing to be married, as we embrace singleness for the present. One channel for loving may be blocked, but plenty of others are open. The gift of celibacy is not earned but it is maintained by the power of the will and by steps of faith. Choosing to receive the gift to serve God results in a supernatural impartation of grace to enable us to walk according to our calling.

In my life, I can see a process of accepting singleness through a series of stages, different at different ages. I made a definite choice to delay marriage in my early twenties. Later I acknowledged my desire to be married while surrendering my right to marriage. I then came to a place of embracing rather than enduring singleness and then eventually to a positive decision not to seek marriage. When I accepted singleness as part of God's calling it involved recognising not just the positive opportunity of being single for God, but making a choice to receive the gift of celibacy as a 'good gift', not a second-rate one.

As Christians, we can recognise that we are single because we have made choices, coming out of our determination not to compromise. We pay a price to live for God, and seek first His Kingdom. Singleness therefore results not just from circumstances but from a willingness to take the risk of renouncing marriage for the sake of the Kingdom.

We must recognise there are no limitations to what single people can do for God, on account of their single state. There may be some boundaries, but these exist for married people too, and we need to embrace boundaries as God-given—to see the difference between boundaries and barriers, between limitations and frustrations. Singleness requires sacrifice, but so does marriage, and all are called to live a holy life for God.

Singleness offers the benefits of a unique opportunity to abandon ourselves to serve God, in undivided devotion, uncluttered, free from distraction, to give Him the very best, by submitting our singleness to His sovereignty.

Thank God for singleness—for tomorrow you may be married!

Thank God for marriage—for tomorrow you may be single!

PART TWO

There are many issues common to all single
people and this section outlines some of
these, to help us to make an appropriate
response to the challenges of singleness.

CHAPTER 5

IDENTITY

Most of us find our identity linked to someone else—we are introduced as 'A's wife' or ' B's son' or 'C's mother', or even 'the pastor's daughter'. How therefore does that leave the single adult? Am I a non-person? Am I 50% of a potential couple? Am I less of a human being? The real question of identity is to do with 'Who am I?' not 'Whose am I?' (i.e. 'Who do I belong to?')

Society, and even the church, sometimes give very low status and apparent stigma to people on their own, which leads to self-doubt and a lack of self-respect, a feeling that I am not valued for myself, but my value is attached to that of someone else. Married couples may refer to 'my other half' and the single person may therefore feel incomplete, as 'one' is not seen as a whole number. Having to go it alone produces feelings of worthlessness and a focus on who I am *not* or what I *don't* have. A sense of being a non-person is only reinforced by well-meaning questions or comments expressing disbelief about one's unmarried state, and so most single people battle with feelings of inadequacy and failure which result in insecurity and inferiority. Thus the question of identity is a threatening one.

Low self-esteem may lead to self-pity, which can easily turn to bitterness or resentment towards others. All of these negative emotions are a result of thinking that is shaped by the pressures of society or of past experiences. It is vital that single men and women find an understanding of God, of themselves and of God's purpose—that they discover their identity in Christ. We need the Holy Spirit to reveal the truth of our position in Christ, to renew our thinking so that we understand that true identity and security are only found in relationship with Him.

Single people have no fixed point from which to work out identity other than the truth from God's Word about being accepted, complete and capable of loving and of being loved. Other relationships may shape our identity but first and foremost our identity is from Jesus. Consider Jesus' response to the Sadducees' questioning (Luke 20:27–40). The Sadducees clearly implied that the woman's identity was tied to her marital status—Jesus turns their question around by teaching that He sees us all as individuals. I like being *just a person* without the label of 'single'.

It is important to develop an understanding of the sovereignty of God, His total commitment to us as individuals and His faithfulness. Developing a personal relationship with God is the foundation from which every issue relating to singleness can be faced. An image of second-class citizenship is often so ingrained that single people find it hard to believe that they have a worthwhile contribution to make. We need to know therefore that our value is in *who* we are, not in our potential usefulness.

The importance of developing a positive self-image and knowing our identity is that, as we discover our own worth and accept the value God places on us, we will also discover the worth of others.

CHAPTER 6

LIFESTYLE

1. Freedom

Single life is uncharted. The single person is free to decide what to do and where to go.

Free to choose
Single people do not necessarily have more time, but do have greater *flexibility* and sometimes greater mobility. Single people still have all the jobs to be done in the home, but they have the freedom to make spontaneous decisions, to choose how to use their time. Those without family responsibilities can drop everything and go.

Free to serve
Paul saw the single life as a life of freedom and availability. This is a challenge for single people to use their freedom to go out and do things that a married person could not do because of family responsibilities. Writing to the Corinthian church (1 Cor. 7), Paul points out that single people are free to give themselves wholly to the work of God, whilst the married person must put the concerns of their spouse and family first. The single person may be free to serve God in places where it might be impractical for families to travel.

Free to love
Freedom is not just practical in terms of time, resources and gifts, home and family responsibilities, but spiritual in terms of devotion to God and capacity to give and receive love. I have read of celibacy described as 'love

wasted on God'. The value of celibacy is compared to the woman in John 12:3 who poured the expensive perfume and her love on Jesus. He placed worth on something which the disciples considered to be worthless—her extravagant expression of love. Single people are capable of wholehearted, undistracted devotion to God and free to *waste* their love on God or, in the words of Paul, free to give God 'undivided devotion' (1 Cor. 7:35). They have unparalleled opportunities to love God and to develop a wide range of relationships because no *one* person has right of access to that love.

Freedom and responsibility
Freedom is to be appreciated and enjoyed, but we must be aware that it can lead to independence and to a self-centred lifestyle. Most younger single people do not have the responsibilities of a family and are therefore free to spend time on themselves. Singles have freedom which can be valued or wasted. They may be free of family responsibilities but freedom does carry a responsibility—the responsibility to choose: to use time, to take initiative, to decide where to live or where to travel, to develop a range of interests and friendships, to be busy or not to be busy!

It is important to learn to balance the necessity of independence with the desire for dependence on God and accountability to others, so that we are choosing freedom in order to serve the Kingdom, not to escape the responsibilities of marriage.

2. Home

Our homes provide an important and God-given opportunity to practise hospitality and to develop friendships. Homemaking is part of the creative nature of both men and women. Enjoying our homes, be it one room or a whole house, is a positive way of expressing our sexuality.

Single people need a home, to put roots down and to feel a sense of permanence and belonging. Yet many single people do not see their house or room as home, but simply as a temporary place to sleep and eat when they can be bothered. Others who live with families can still feel like rootless lodgers.

Single people together can make a house into a home, but they are often used to thinking only of themselves and being independent. A desire for home and committed friendships requires laying down some of that independence. Many single people co-exist in houses, rather than work through the cost and inconvenience of sharing lives and making a real home. Sometimes one single person may own the home and carry all the responsibility, with another single person as a lodger, yet others may assume that single people living together are sharing responsibilities. This can be a great pressure on the home-owner and clear communication is essential for people living together.

Most single people setting up home do not have the benefits of wedding presents to furnish it or, following separation, they may have lost many or all of their furnishings. In addition, the responsibilities of running a home, with no one to share the work load, are emotionally, as well as physically, demanding. Many household tasks require two pairs of hands. Offers of help are valued, especially by those who are seeking to be self-sufficient and 'cope' alone. For example: how do I manage to fix up the curtain rail if I have no drill and no one to tell me when it is straight? Without wishing to reinforce gender stereotypes, there are practical implications of running a home alone, with different tasks presenting different problems for men and women. Domestic crises or little emergencies emphasise aloneness.

For practical reasons singles are often seen as those who receive hospitality, but we also need to take on responsibility and make opportunities to give it, accepting our limitations and difficulties. Many single people find it difficult to invite a married couple for dinner, maybe fearing that the couple would prefer not to spend time with a 'one' person. Another mindset to be broken is the fear of taking sole responsibility for getting the meal and acting as host alone. This can be especially difficult for those who have been used to sharing the responsibility for entertaining with a partner, or for whom the model from upbringing is a shared task. It takes a lot of confidence to entertain alone and sometimes more than can be mustered.

Single people are an embarrassment at dinner parties because they make an uneven number and many married people restrict their invitations to couples. Single people get invited to tea with the children, or otherwise an unattached member of the opposite sex is also invited. This can put pressure on the single person, either because they wonder if there is some matchmaking intention, or feel that they have been invited just to make even numbers! It is actually OK to invite a single person on their own whatever society says.

Jesus broke through all the cultural barriers of His day. He sat with women, He ate with women, He accepted a drink from a prostitute, He relaxed in the home with single men and women. Does it matter if an uneven number sit round the table or if there is an unbalanced ratio of men to women? Who is setting the rules? Extended families and single people making a home together are a positive and a challenging illustration of the gospel to the world, but they can also be misunderstood or viewed with suspicion. *Let's be mould breakers.*

3. Work

Employment can be very important for single people, not just as essential breadwinning but to bring a measure of fulfilment. In fact most men and some single women find their identity in their work. There are those who choose to pursue a career rather than marriage, and others who because they have not married, choose a career that meets some of their personal needs. Single people are free to give themselves wholeheartedly, in terms of availability, to their work, without the constraints of family. However, they do need to be careful not to fill all their time with work, leaving none for themselves or to develop friendships.

For many single women the option of pursuing a career can be a real pressure, especially when work is a necessity rather than a chosen vocation. Even today, many women do not go into a job planning a lifetime in a career. For others, looking ahead to retirement can be difficult, especially when their work has provided a major source of fulfilment and contact with other people.

4. Social scene

The myth of the single social scene needs exploding. Whilst it appears that singles have a particular social life, it is often circumstances that cause single people to gravitate together. I quote from *Two's company, one's an outcast* (Daily Mail, 23/1/90): 'The age of the singles is over. Singles are now the new social lepers: barred from couple-orientated dinner parties, humiliated at company social functions, subjected to probing questions from suspicious aunts.'

We have a challenge to live as a radical community, overcoming those 'world' concepts which make single people unacceptable and uncomfortable in a social setting. When our workplace invites us to bring a partner to social events, are we expected to go with a same-sex friend, with someone else's husband or wife, or with a single person of the opposite sex? How do we cope with the insinuations? Alternatively, do we help the single person to feel positive about the pressure of going alone? If married people are invited with a free place for their spouse, why shouldn't the single person get a free place for a friend? Prejudice and discrimination against the single person are seen in these kinds of situations.

Times of celebration such as birthdays, Christmas, weddings and births can be the most painful for people on their own, highlighting their 'oneness' and their lack of someone special with whom to share these significant occasions. Engagements, weddings, births and special wedding anniversaries are occasions where individuals are treated with special honour. The single person misses out on these opportunities for being the focus of attention and being 'honoured'. It falls to the single person to arrange their own 'milestone' birthday celebrations, which again underlines aloneness.

Holidays too can pose a nightmare for the single person. Even the church family holiday can sometimes reinforce feelings of isolation—who will share the chalet or room? Holidays can be an ideal opportunity for families and single people to consider spending time together, the single person delighting in being organised and cared for, and not having the responsibility for making all the arrangements. There are other single people who would prefer to be away from a family and the demands of children. (So would many parents but they have sacrificed that choice!)

Sundays can be very lonely days for single people and even the church meeting can be the very place where a single person's sense of being alone is reinforced. A person can arrive alone and then go back home alone after a meeting, while longing for an invitation to join others over a drink together. Single people are often either the last to hang around at the end of meetings for this reason, or the first to leave to avoid feeling rejected and lonely!

Feelings of vulnerability intensify when practical or emotional support is not forthcoming. Family relationships in the church have enormous potential to help or to hinder these situations.

CHAPTER 7

RELATIONSHIPS

Another key in responding to singleness is to develop meaningful relationships, but this can be a difficult area for many single people. God has made us for companionship—loving and being loved are basic needs of every human being.

Loneliness is often a very painful reality for all single people, more acute at some ages and stages in life. Long periods alone easily lead to self-pity and link with rejection and a lack of self-love. This results in difficulty both in giving and receiving love. It is so easy to fall into the trap of thinking that marriage is the answer to loneliness, and that if I were married I would never be lonely. It is generally true that single people face loneliness more than married people, since there is no one person there specially for them. Figures from the Marriage Research Centre at the Central Middlesex Hospital show that suicide rates for single men are three times higher than for married men, and for single women twice as high as for married women. Being alone in a world of couples is not easy—couples do have each other to depend on, but God does not leave the single person to cope on their own. The challenge when facing loneliness is to decide where to turn: in on ourselves, or to God and others.

Aloneness and *loneliness* are very different. Aloneness is physical and loneliness is psychological— it is possible to be alone and not to feel lonely. We all, single and married, need to find the freedom to accept aloneness at times. There are two ways of viewing every situation: time alone can be a precious gift, or a painful, unwanted state. We can choose to feel sorry for ourselves or learn to appreciate the positive aspects of being alone.

However, there is a difference between choosing to be alone and being forced by circumstances to be alone. The latter may lead to a state of independence leading on to isolation. Aloneness hurts when we realise that we are no one's priority, when there is no one special to turn to for advice, or as a sounding board, no one for feedback or comments, for sharing decisions, no one to bring a balance or an objective perspective. This is especially acute for those living alone, although it is also possible to live with others and experience the same pangs of aloneness, for loneliness is not always dispelled by company. Loneliness can be particularly acute at night, when married people have each other.

Single people can feel or become isolated as a result of hurts in previous relationships if they withdraw in order to survive. Lack of contact with others can tend towards self-orientation which in turn leads to introspection. A sense of isolation can be accompanied by feelings of anger, frustration or self-pity, and is sometimes exacerbated by added feelings of guilt or failure.

As we accept ourselves and our current situation, we need to be prepared to take some risks and initiate change. An answer to loneliness is to share ourselves with others: love has two aspects—receiving and giving—and we need both. All relationships carry the potential for disappointment and hurt. Single people can be reluctant to pursue relationships because of fear of the risks involved, and of feeling vulnerable. Trusting others is extremely difficult, especially for many single people who carry rejection and hurt caused by a history of failed relationships. We have a choice—to live in isolation with the hurt or to give ourselves away.

There are two responses to rejection and failure in relationships : one is withdraw and remain in self-pity, the other is to respond to the healing love of God, and find a place of self-acceptance. In the context of the church, healing can be experienced and a sense of security discovered that will enable the single person to belong: in church and in society. Becoming part of family in the church involves letting go of our independence, allowing God into our lives, facing the truth about ourselves, recognising our need of other people and being willing to take risks and to be inconvenienced at times. True friendship is a gift from God, and brings fulfilment. Single people are free to build friendships, but there is a cost—of giving self, time and effort.

All single people have an enormous capacity for loving which can be locked up and wasted. Building relationships takes time. We need to face our feelings of anger or disappointment and find the way of forgiveness. God does not promise marriage but He does promise love. He is a God of compassion and '[his] unfailing love for you will not be shaken' (Is. 54:10).

The Bible is clear that we are made to be in relationship—'It is not good for the man to be alone'(Gen. 2:18). Ecclesiastes 4:9–12 speaks of the difficulties facing the loner. 'Two are better than one . . . If one falls down his friend can help him up. But pity the man who falls and has no-one to help him up! . . . Though one may be overpowered, two can defend themselves.' In these passages there is nothing to suggest that the two are necessarily a man and a woman in a marriage relationship. The principle of, and need for, relationship applies equally to married and single people. Sometimes in the church we can perceive it as a weakness to admit our need for friendship, thinking it is more spiritual to say that Jesus meets all our needs. He does, but He has given us a body in which to give and receive love, to care for and support each other, as a way of knowing and sharing His love.

It is important that the church allows us, men as well as women, to admit our need for companionship. All of us need people with whom to share our successes and those special moments of pleasure—not just our difficulties and sad times. Finding friends to share our grief and our joys with can bring healing. The community of the church involves single and married people *together*, giving and receiving love, prepared to be open and honest with each other, accepting one another and willing to be vulnerable. In developing relationships we need to see people as people, not as the means to fulfil our needs. We all need friendship to receive encouragement and to be open for correction as well.

Relationships in the church family can be liberating, as married people share their lives and their children with single people, and singles bring their world into the family home.The church has a great opportunity to model an environment of trust allowing affection to be expressed, free of suspicion, demonstrating honesty and integrity in relationships. The basis of all healthy relationships is first of all our relationship with God, and the strength of this will enable us to develop *Christ-centred* friendships. Whilst we might all like to focus our love on just one person, we do have the opportunity as single people to share our love in a variety of ways which will bring richness to our lives.

The church should aim to promote and encourage deep relationships between single and married people. We need to see the barriers broken down—often feelings of anger or frustration cause invisible walls of envy, suspicion or even hostility between single and married people. We must recognise the need for repentance of any envy of the status or circumstances of others and see each other as men and women who are made in the image of God—all one in Christ Jesus. The foundation on which close extended family friendships can be developed is that of total commitment to the sanctity of marriage, and awareness of the potential difficulties in sharing lives together. Sadly, fear of unhealthy attraction between a single person and a married member of the opposite sex has at times allowed the enemy to rob the church of Kingdom relationships, as modelled by Jesus and the New Testament church.

The church has a powerful message of unity in all its diversity. It can demonstrate what Kingdom family really means. The church needs single people of all ages and experiences to live out its message of reconciliation and relationship. Maintaining a variety of friendships in the church is very important and needs to be worked at. Most people accept that marriage requires commitment and time, and single people also need to give time to developing quality friendships.

1. Men with men; women with women

God wants to restore our understanding of the depth of same-gender friendship in a way that will be liberating for many single men and women. David and Jonathan, Ruth and Naomi, and Jesus and John modelled this kind of friendship but Satan has distorted what God had planned—the characteristics of trust and openness, of laying lives down for each other, of showing respect and understanding, and a willingness to sacrifice. Single people's underutilised capacity to give and receive love can be expressed through friendships. So often close friendship with the same gender is marred by prejudice—our western culture views deep companionship, especially between two men, with suspicion. Friendship that does not involve sexual expression is perceived as exceptional and abnormal.

David and Jonathan made a covenant of genuine love which was not of a sexual nature. 'Jonathan became one in spirit with David, and he loved him as himself' (1 Sam. 18:1). Jonathan took the initiative and the two men made a pledge of friendship which God used for His purposes. The friendship of David and Jonathan involved commitment, and the freedom to share their lives and show affection without emotional dependency or eroticism: 'They kissed each other and wept together' (1 Sam. 20:41.) Their friendship was marked by loyalty and a desire to help each other to grow in God, and to support and protect each other unconditionally. We read of David bowing down to Jonathan as a sign of submission and respect, and they made a covenant together 'before the Lord'. Jonathan helped David 'to find strength in God' (1 Sam. 23:16) and from this base they were free to express their love.

Jesus and John: Jesus too had a special bond of love with John, who is called many times in John's Gospel 'the disciple whom Jesus loved'.

The relationship between *Ruth and Naomi* is again characterised by qualities of trust and honesty, respect and understanding. Neither is driven by their emotional needs, yet they are free to express affection. Their loyalty and commitment are expressed in these words: 'Where you go I will go, and where you stay, I will stay' (Ruth 1:16). Within that commitment there was also the freedom to release each other, which we see outworked when Ruth is released by Naomi to get married.

Generally, our society does not allow for this depth of friendship which presents a challenge if the church is to model and encourage covenant friendships other than marriage. Committed friendship brings opportunities to love, to share weaknesses and disappointments as well as successes, joys and all the pleasure of companionship. However, no deep friendship will develop without a willingness to embrace the sacrifice that is involved in commitment. It is especially important to pray for protection in close friendships—they can be a target for suspicion and misunderstanding as the enemy will seek to destroy what God has redeemed. Deep friendships will lead to feelings of affection and the potential for sin always exists. We always need to guard against emotional dependency and exclusiveness in such relationships. Idolatry begins where the friendship, rather than Jesus, becomes the means of life support. It is unhealthy to concentrate all our emotional energy on one person and we need to be careful of jealousy in friendships. However, we should not be afraid of covenant friendships. The suspicion of others can restrict the single person from pursuing healthy loving relationships. God's creative plan for such relationships are a powerful statement of His redeeming love and grace.

It is helpful to encourage the single person to pursue a broad base of friendships, to ensure that a 'covenant friendship' does not result in over-dependency on one person, and subsequent loss of freedom to live in 'undivided devotion' as described by Paul. A covenant relationship between two men, or two women, is *not* marriage, even though much of their lives are shared; there is no physical union and the two are still separate with no exclusive rights to each other. Only in marriage is there this oneness, as the husband and wife have been joined in a one-flesh union, and therefore have given unique rights to each other.

2. Men with women

Single people also need mixed company. A 'women's night out' may be a treat for mothers, but can be a chore for single women who socialise mainly with other single women! The key questions are:

- Is the single person able to find companionship with the opposite sex?
- Is it possible for men and women to enjoy any depth of committed friendship without romantic love? C. S. Lewis in *The Four Loves* suggests that a depth of friendship between the two sexes will almost certainly pass into erotic love.

With a mature self-awareness and in accountability, a depth of relationship is not only possible, but part of God's plan for a redeemed and prophetic community. We need to share lives together in integrity and trust, expressing femininity and masculinity in healthy and creative ways, as a way of restoring and reflecting the creative image of God. This surely is part of the freedom that Christ has bought for us. Jesus not only teaches about the value of friendship: He models it. He was not afraid to build close friendships with both men and women. John describes how Jesus displayed emotion in His relationship with Mary, Martha and Lazarus.

Healthy male-female friendships bring an affirmation and enjoyment of sexuality. We need to acknowledge that in any relationship a sexual dynamic exists because we are sexual beings. What happens when one person feels romantic or sexual love for the other, and this is either not reciprocated or inappropriate? The fear of this scenario stops many men and women from pursuing friendships. Wisdom, together with transparency and accountability, is essential in all our relationships.

The more a single person has accepted and embraced their singleness, the more free they will be to enjoy friendships with people of both sexes, regardless of marital status. Sometimes single people are perceived to be a greater risk in working with members of the opposite sex, and given a stricter set of guidelines. Experience has shown that single people often have far *greater* awareness of these risks than many married people.

The church needs to view friendships between two single people of opposite sexes with understanding and sensitivity, encouraging men and women to relate together as people, not as potential marriage partners. Single people need the support and understanding of the church in developing and enjoying genuine friendships, men with women, and women with men. This should not spark inappropriate discussion, unhelpful speculation or interference. These things immediately put a friendship under pressure and can jeopardise its further development.

Single people value and enjoy relationships with both sexes where there is mutual respect and responsibility in the way we treat one another. If we see marriage as the only goal, it becomes the hidden motive behind everything. If we pursue marriage rather than love, we spoil the naturalness in friendship and affect the development of relationships with the opposite sex.

3. Single people with families

Single people can find another dimension in relationships by involvement in families, and outworking the scriptural promise that 'God sets the lonely in families'(Ps. 68:6). Family is a helpful context in which to develop friendships, to find companionship with men and women, and with children. Many welcome the diversity of family friendships, rather than 'singles groups'. Meals with married couples can be a real treat for many—an opportunity to be treated as adults, and to enjoy the pleasure of mixed company. A single person may find it difficult to initiate a relationship with a couple, for fear of being intrusive, or because of an assumption that couples prefer to spend time with other couples. However, by sharing lives together both the family and the single person will be enriched in a way that brings wholeness and fulfilment. They will stand as another prophetic statement to society.

I want to illustrate this with my own story of one such family. This family opened their home and their lives to me, and I enjoyed all the privileges and the responsibilities of being part of their home and family life. Within that context I was free to offer to look after the children and to serve in practical ways, especially as I did not have a home of my own at the time, and was free of householding responsibilities. They were also free to ask me to serve them, seeing me as more than a useful resource for babysitting so that they could be out at meetings. It took time and effort, and there was a cost involved, but there were rich rewards.

Their marriage was strong and secure enough to welcome me into it, for the wife not to feel threatened by me, and for me to feel safe with either or both. They trusted me enough to give me the children for days or weekends so that they could have time on their own. They were prepared to give away their privacy and it was a real privilege to share lives together, with no secret areas. It was also an honour to be close to a Christian marriage, to be included in it, sharing the good times and the conflicts, and learning about giving and commitment in relationship, as God intended it.

I was able to make a contribution into the family so that the relationship was not just fulfilling *my* needs. I was able to bring my 'outside' world, particularly for the wife and mother who was temporarily focused on home and babies. It was always important to show tact and sensitivity when they needed time alone, and by open talking the level of trust all round was deepened. I was concerned not to abuse the privilege and spoil the friendship, and recognised I had no right other than what they gave to me.

4. Children

The friendship of children can bring special opportunities for love and affection to be given and received in the lives of single people. They communicate acceptance in quite unique ways and can be a great help in times of loneliness, as well as providing outlets for maternal and paternal feelings. Single people can have a significant role with children, providing positive role models through their friendship—as one child was heard to say: 'I don't have to marry when I grow up, I think I'll be like Sally'(the single adult living in their family). Single people can be encouraged to look for opportunities where they can enjoy the privilege of investing their lives in particular children.

Elderly people on their own welcome the company of 'adopted' children and grandchildren, especially where they have no family of their own. It is also a great challenge to the church to be providing good and balanced models of relationships to children of single parents.

5. Parents

An understanding of the spiritual dynamic of *leaving and cleaving* is helpful for single people in relationship with their parents. Jesus quoting Genesis 2:24 makes it clear that leaving father and mother is necessary in order to cleave to a spouse (Matt. 19:5). Apart from failing to meet their expectations in terms of marriage, many single people have not *left* their parents emotionally. This can result in inordinate demands on single people from parents, with far higher expectations being placed on them than on married brothers and sisters. The pressure of parents on single people can be controlling and manipulative. The words 'bachelor' or 'spinster' are sometimes used as descriptive terms for those who are not free of their parents, and who therefore carry some responsibility for them.

Single people need to find release from their parents in order to be free to honour them and serve them. This pressure becomes particularly acute when facing increasing age in parents, with their failing health, and eventual death. Society generally assumes that the single adult without children has a greater obligation to care for their ageing parent(s) than married people, who have family commitments. We need to be aware of the expectations of people on their own in carrying these responsibilities and face the implications for the church family.

Many single adults have never grown up, are still treated as children by their parents, and depend on them emotionally. We must encourage the relationship to change so that we can honour and respect our parents, but not be subject to them. Then, and only then, we will be free to care for them out of choice, not from emotional pressure.

There are older single people, particularly women,

who never left home, and as their parents became dependent, were then not free to leave. By default therefore, they sacrificed marriage out of a duty to care for their parents. This often results in tremendous loneliness when their parents die because they have been isolated from developing a range of friendships. It is also important to understand the fear in many single people of growing older alone and to acknowledge the need to care for older single people both in the church, and in our communities.

The increasing emphasis in recent legislation on the role of communities and families to care for their elderly relatives is a return to the biblical culture of extended families—a culture still prevalent in many 'two-thirds world' countries. This presents a tremendous challenge and opportunity for the church to offer friendship and practical support to many elderly people living alone, who have no families to care for them and who can feel neglected.

CHAPTER 8

INTIMACY AND SEXUALITY

Intimacy

The desire for affection—to be *'the most important person to someone, somewhere, sometime'*—is extremely real for every human being, although often acknowledged more by women than men. Intimacy is about someone being there when you need them, often for a hug, sometimes just for undivided attention, to be someone's priority, just to be 'special'. As we have already seen, Paul (1 Cor. 7:4) teaches that husband and wife have exclusive rights to each other's bodies which single people will not have of another person.

All human beings have a need for emotional intimacy and we need to recognise the importance of touch in affirming and strengthening friendship. Touch is an essential ingredient in life and it is powerful in bringing comfort and healing to sick people. Many single people are deprived of the display of affection communicated by touch and suffer 'skin hunger'! But some associate touch with fear because of distorted experiences. Society distorts intimacy and affection, always linking it with sex. Most single people struggle more with their desire for emotional intimacy and affection than for sex itself, although sex is frequently perceived as the main need. If our basic human needs for love and belonging are met, the sex drive is often less of a problem. Sadly, some single people find their longing for affection so intolerable that they rush into marriage looking to receive (rather than to give) affection. They end up disillusioned.

It is in this area of intimacy that a single person's relationship with God is very important—knowing consolation in loneliness and healing when rejection and hurt cause pain. It is really only God who can meet our deepest needs for intimacy. Jesus demonstrated union in His relationship with His father: 'I and the Father are one'(John 10:30); and Paul describes this same 'intimacy' with God when he writes: 'I no longer live, but Christ lives in me'(Gal. 2:20).

Nevertheless, all single people need close friendship and affection expressed, with and without touch, as a fulfilment of the basic human need to belong. Relationships in the church family can help to meet this need, and to provide a measure of spiritual intimacy, especially where sexual intimacy is lacking. Affection is not just to do with physical expression, it is about expressing a person's worth and value, uniqueness and significance. The powerful media message is that sex is *the* answer to loneliness and it is therefore no wonder that loneliness and sexuality are the most common issues faced by single people.

Sexuality

We live in a sex-mad society which shouts the message that sexual activity is a moral right. Almost every magazine and every film has a message about sex, overtly or by implication. The church has, in the main, been silent, or restricted its teaching on sex to 'marrieds' or a 'pre-marriage' chat.

What is the culture surrounding single people?
In the '90s, sex between unmarried people is normal, acceptable and fashionable. AIDS has addressed promiscuity but not promoted total abstinence. Sexual abstinence is seen as freakish and generally impossible, virginity is seen as laughable or unattractive and many single people are ashamed to be virgins. Celibacy is an

old-fashioned word and the concept is unacceptable. There was a quote, from the *Dictionary of Quotations*, in a Daily Mail article (29/5/92) on celibacy, which said that 'celibacy has no pleasure'. To be sexually inactive is considered boring, narrow and cold. Chastity (i.e. abstinence from sex outside marriage, and faithfulness in marriage) is definitely out of line with the culture of the '90s. Immoral sexual activity makes headline news. Society says sex equals fulfilment of the need to belong and to be loved, and virginity equals the opposite. The secular attitude (particularly for men) is: 'If it feels good, do it!' Freud describes those who live in a state of sexual abstinence as socially retarded, unbalanced and disturbed—not an accurate description of Jesus and Paul!

Virginity is given away in a moment often because of an unwillingness to stand up and be different. But the media pressure is powerful and the biblical standard of sexual morality is seen as restrictive and undesirable. The television, films, music, etc. all stimulate our sexual appetite, but for the single person there is no outlet for those desires to be fulfilled. The church needs to give a relevant lead in presenting an attractive and possible alternative.

Sex in the God-appointed context of marriage is beautiful; outside the God-given boundaries, it causes untold damage. God created sex to be an expression of the total giving of a man to a woman and a woman to a man, with affirmation of self-worth, intimacy and a unique sense of belonging. The media distortion portrays sex as a goal in itself, promoting the lie that sex is the answer to loneliness. Experience shows that sex outside the context of a loving, committed relationship increases feelings of low value, of rejection and of being discarded.

God places limits on our sexual behaviour, but not on the expression of sexuality. The problem is that the world has limited our understanding of sexuality to be sexual intercourse. Sexuality, that is our masculinity and femininity, is expressed in all that we are and do, but

Satan has totally distorted it. Because the image of God is in our sexuality, the effects of sin and deception are huge. It is important to develop a Kingdom understanding of sexuality and to know God's work of redemption.

Single people are not sexless beings, but men and women with the same sexual energy as married people. The church has often denied single people a positive approach to embracing and expressing our sexuality. We need to understand that sexuality is God's gift—to thank Him for it and enjoy it, rather than seeing it as an unwelcome burden to be done away with. Sexuality can be the hardest aspect of singleness in a society where personal identity is closely linked with sexual behaviour. Most single people who struggle with their sexual longings are actually looking for acceptance and belonging. They believe the lie that sexual intercourse is *the* answer, yet expressing our sexuality as men and women is far more than fulfilment of the sexual drive. The answer lies in finding ways of embracing sexuality and practical helps to rejecting immorality.

The church can encourage single people to see themselves as sexual beings and not to feel guilty about acknowledging their sexuality. Sometimes single people find it difficult to acknowledge their sexual feelings in case they are perceived as unspiritual. The intense feeling that something is wrong with them can lead single people to question their femininity or masculinity, and lead them to deny their feelings altogether. Denial can actually cause an exaggeration of sexual feelings, and lead to unhealthy addiction. The reluctance of some married people, or churches, to discuss any aspect of sex in front of single people can serve to reinforce the feeling that single people are abnormal.

Coming to terms with our sexual identity is essential, but living with celibacy is difficult because it involves denial of a natural God-given drive. However, surrendering our sexuality (including our sexual desires) to God can enable a release of energy in other ways. Many single people who have embraced celibacy have a very healthy and balanced awareness of their own sexuality and have much to offer both married and single people.

Single people may see their sexuality as a great burden especially if they have had sexual experience. Previous sexual experience, be it good or bad, will influence their ability to come to terms with their sexuality and adjust to celibacy. We need to recognise the bereavement process for those who have been in good intimate relationships—the tensions and feelings of loss and waste they experience. John White describes celibacy as 'sexual fasting' and suggests that like fasting from food, it becomes easier with practice. He advocates 'practising the habit of celibacy' to train our bodies to manage without sex, which he says, is possible even if painful. I would add to this that, for most single people, celibacy requires *relinquishment* of the expression of sexual desires rather than fasting, since fasting is usually for a defined period.

Our attitude to sexuality and to sexual abstinence is extremely important—if our minds are constantly focusing on our need for sex, then sexual abstinence will prove an impossible standard, and become an obsession. It is said that 90% of sex is in the mind, which is why Paul's exhortation to 'take captive every thought to make it obedient to Christ' (2 Cor. 10:5) is so relevant in the area of sexual desires. Fantasy can be a powerful and addictive way of escaping from reality. Julia Duin in *Sex and the Single Christian* underlines the importance of controlling the mind. She compares reading sexually stimulating material while trying to remain celibate, to reading a gourmet magazine while trying to diet.

Single people need to understand that sexual desires in themselves are not wrong, and God has given us a way of ensuring these do not become an overwhelming frustration. The issue is one of controlling our mind and our will rather than letting our desires control us. He has promised the Holy Spirit to help us, and self-control is a fruit of the Spirit which we need to allow to grow in our lives. It is helpful to understand the war between the flesh and the spirit. The spirit may be willing but the flesh is designed to work in a very different direction! Many single men and women struggle with masturbation, and feel guilty about finding it a helpful way to release sexual energy. Although the Bible is silent on the subject of masturbation, the same principles outlined above concerning fantasy and obsession are relevant.

Maintaining biblical standards of sexual morality does produce tension and conflict. We need to face up honestly to our feelings and to the strength of our emotional and physical desires, knowing God understands our deepest longings, and can meet the very deepest of our needs.

Wise counsel to single people battling with their sexual desires involves positive channelling of those energies in creative ways, and encouragement on how to guard their affections. A message of 'don't', or 'you must not', or even relevant Scriptures, leads to denial or repression of sexual feelings, and a feeling of waste. Single people need practical advice, not 'pious platitudes'. Meditating on God, or praying about it, is not always the most helpful advice in the midst of intense struggles or even vague longings. Asking God to take away sexual desires is asking Him to contravene His creation; prayer for self-control is very effective alongside practical activity to distract.

Single people need to understand the link between spirituality and sexuality, and to know that we have access to the grace of God to enable us to present our bodies as a living sacrifice, holy and pleasing to God, not conformed to this world (Rom. 12:1–2). As we discover that God's will is acceptable and surrender our sexual desires to Him, we will find victory and peace.

The shortage of single men in churches can cause single women to look elsewhere if they are struggling with their own desire for affection and intimacy. For many single women in a business environment, there is no shortage of opportunities. Talking about our vulnerable areas with people we trust will help to bring a sense of accountability, which can enable us to face and overcome these pressures. Clear open decisions and predetermined choices can help when the single person is faced with temptation. In times of vulnerability we need to guard our affections with an awareness of appropriate boundaries. Having no unshared areas in our lives is a great safety valve.

Although the biblical standard of sexual abstinence outside marriage is high, and, according to society, outdated—clearly it is possible. Jesus was 'tempted in every way, just as we are—yet was without sin' (Hebrews 4:15). We too are free not to have sex, but this requires a choice. Celibacy is not easy but it is possible with God's grace.

The church can help, encourage and support those who are seeking to adhere to biblical standards of morality, to cope with the pressures of swimming against the tide. We need to help single people to think through issues relating to their gender identity and their sexuality, and to find positive ways to channel emotions and demonstrate affection without compromise. It takes courage to be different, but there is no other option for the single Christian—God requires purity.

But what if we step over the boundaries?

Negative messages, or even silence, can place a weight of shame and guilt on those who have succumbed to temptation or indulged in fantasy. Many single Christians endure crippling struggles in the areas of sexual shame and guilt (false or real) because they feel unable to share them. Sometimes it seems as though sexual sin is discussed more in relation to marital faithfulness than to sexual abstinence.

The church is the agent of healing, bringing God's forgiveness and cleansing to people weighed down with the shame and guilt of sexual sin, or sometimes the false guilt attached to what they perceive to be sin (e.g.

masturbation). It is a challenge to consider our attitudes to sexual sin and sexual deviances, to ensure that there is no condemnation of the person. Sexual sin is no worse than any other sin in God's eyes, but it is different. Paul describes sexual sin as self-gratifying and against one's own body, and therefore the consequences are usually more damaging. We need to extend God's grace to see single people acknowledge their need for repentance and experience release from the guilt and shame of sexual sin. Becoming a new creation includes restored virginity.

A high-trust environment

The Bible promotes celibacy as a positive alternative lifestyle, yet historically, the church has not generally addressed this, except in religious orders. The church needs to create an environment of high trust and acceptance, to encourage openness and honesty in relationships with appropriate guidelines on pastoral care for men and women. It needs to show under-standing, acknowledge the reality of temptations and pressures, and emphasise the positive aspects of sexual abstinence and sexual intercourse.

Forums for teaching and discussion on a biblical understanding of sexuality can be helpful. In a safe environment, single people can be encouraged to share not only their struggles but also their perspectives on positive ways to embrace sexuality. We need to exercise wisdom regarding the mix of those attending and appropriate people to lead these discussions in constructive and helpful ways. Sometimes talking about sex can become an unhealthy substitute for doing it!

It is important to understand that, for some single men and women from a homosexual background, celibacy may be the only option open to them on account of their sexual orientation. The church needs to offer support and understanding as they embrace the process of healing. Others who, on account of physical or mental disabilities are incapable of sexual intercourse, may need help in accepting their celibate lifestyle.

The new dynamism of the '90s could be sexual abstinence. It could release a whole new spiritual power, addressing the forces of darkness that have distorted the God-ordained foundation of sexual intercourse as the pinnacle of expression of love and commitment. The church has a theology that is radical. We totally oppose the world's view as we present celibacy as a possible way of life and virginity as a priceless quality, especially when we choose to turn our backs on 'sex' and give our energies to serving God.

CHAPTER 9

LOSS

Single again

Most of this Pioneer *Perspective* addresses issues related to anyone who is single today, for whatever reason. However, I want to address, in brief, some very specific areas concerning those who find themselves single after a period of marriage. The church needs to develop an understanding of divorcees, of single parents, and of widows/widowers—looking for opportunities to be inclusive. These people are not problems, or a threat to family life.

For men and women who find themselves single again, the main issue is adjustment, usually sudden, to life without a partner, to being a 'one' having been used to sharing as half of a couple. Becoming single again can be totally devastating, especially if it is unexpected. People need time to adjust to the gap that is left—to the implications of a new role in society and in the church, and changes in lifestyle, from dependence to enforced independence. The emptiness of finding yourself alone, of feeling trapped with no one to turn to and no way out, can be shattering.

For people who have been married or cohabited, there is the adjustment at a practical level to being on your own: no more shared decision-making; the expectations of who does what, once established, have now changed; often financial pressures have implications on home and lifestyle; the pressure of being both mother and father to the children, of being both husband and wife around the home; and the pressure of needing to go to work to earn money but being needed at home by the children.

Divorce still carries a stigma. Emotions range from guilt to shame, from humiliation to anger, from resentment to hurt, mixed in with a sense of failure and inadequacy. All of these need to be faced up to and expressed. Some divorcees may never have developed their own identity before entering marriage and almost certainly have lost it in the process of their marriage failing. Divorced people can be viewed with fear or suspicion. The separated or divorced female already carries a sense of failure and is often viewed as 'easy to get' by the world. There is great pressure for divorcees to remarry or to find an outlet for sexual expression. It is estimated that one in three divorced people remarry within a couple of years. Maintaining dignity in these circumstances requires courage and faith . . . and the support of friendship.

For people experiencing separation, the adjustment to singleness can be a confusing process, as they still have a marriage partner and so are not really single. They are facing all the issues of singleness without the freedom to work them through.

Most single parents struggle with feelings of inadequacy and rejection. They may at times become overwhelmed by the pressures and demands of bringing up children alone, as well as coping with their personal readjustment to singleness. This is an area where the church can offer practical support such as being aware of boys needing a dad to take an interest in sporting events, or girls needing a mum to discuss growing up, clothes, etc. The church is God's gift to these situations in the shape not just of other families, but of other single people who can be aunts and uncles and fulfil a vital role of support to single parents and their children. Childless single people also benefit in finding an outlet for their drive to nurture children.

Bereavement

Loss can be a devastating experience for single people, not just for those who have been widowed. Any loss of a partner is a kind of death. So too are the realisation that options to marry are decreasing, the disappointment and regret about what should or could have been and the loss of sexual intimacy.

Both sudden loss and the process of loss produce shock and grief. They require a bereavement period involving time to adjust to the loss, time to grieve for what might have been, time to face the implications and time to allow healing to take place. It has been said that bereavement following death takes up to two years, and following divorce up to five years. In a divorce situation the partner is still alive. It is easier to come to terms with the finality of death. Those who find themselves single again need space—to discover their worth and value as people in their own right, to believe in themselves, to find the confidence to do things again (or for the first time), to see themselves as single and to find the courage to accept the gift of singleness.

Childlessness

Coping with strong maternal instincts, as women approach their forties, can lead to anger and resentment, which in turn affect self-image. It is sometimes considered unacceptable for single women to express maternal instincts and face up to the painful reality of childlessness. Coping with the stigma of being childless, as well as not being married, can be intolerable for some women. Motherhood is so powerfully associated with being a true woman that some single women today are deliberately choosing to have children. Men also struggle with paternal instincts, which although not time-linked as for women, can be equally intense, and probably far less acceptable to admit. An understanding that acceptability to God does not depend on marital status or childbearing can prove liberating.

Facing the issues of childlessness or loss of sexual intimacy can become a tremendous pressure, especially if opportunities for relationship arise with non-Christian men or women. The choice to remain single in these circumstances takes great courage and can cause many single people to face a crisis of faith.

The loss of natural children can be helped by the gain of spiritual children and the rewards and sacrifice involved in bringing to birth spiritual babies. Isaiah prophesied into a society where barrenness brought disgrace and shame. His words are a great source of encouragement in facing childlessness.

> "Sing, O barren woman,
>   you who never bore a child;
> burst into song, shout for joy,
>   you who were never in labour;
> because more are the children of the desolate
>   woman
>   than of her who has a husband,"
>   says the Lord
>   (Is. 54:1).

God promises to heal the broken-hearted and bind up their wounds.

PART THREE

CHAPTER 10

CHURCH RESPONSE

Singleness presents an opportunity for response, not a problem for reaction!

How can the church take the initiative in responding to the challenge of the increasing numbers and diversity of single people both in the population at large and in churches? I am grouping my recommendations under four headings:

- *Examine*
- *Envision*
- *Equip and encourage*
- *Evangelise*

Examine

1. Discover what the family of God means—a family that is characterised by acceptance, honesty and order, which relates radically with trust, commitment and purity. Go for the restoration of extended family, of brothers and sisters treating one another with dignity and respect—see the Kingdom alternative to the decaying family in our Western society.

2. Identify who is in the family: the 30-year-old single woman caring for a senile parent, the young widow with her toddler, the divorced man with his teenage daughter, the single man in his thirties who never married, the 45-year-old single woman facing a childless future, the elderly widower, the young men who have lived together in a homosexual relationship, the teenage girl with a baby, the young man with

learning difficulties. Consider the pastoral implications of each of these. In addition, be aware of those who are single at church because their partner is an unbeliever.

3. Examine our attitudes to and perceptions of singleness, in honesty and openness, demonstrating awareness and understanding of the worth and value of single people. Seek to understand the issues so as to ensure that singles are not seen as problems. We need to address the fantasy and face the reality concerning the comparisons of singleness versus marriage, ensuring neither state is viewed with admiration or pity.

4. Ask ourselves if there are ways we can encourage more single people to be in positions of responsibility in the church, and whether any historic trend of 'married housegroup leaders' needs adjustment.

5. Repent where necessary of attitudes of envy, jealousy or resentment—married to single, or single to married. The implications of Jesus' invitation to 'follow me' involves leaving preconceived ideas and prejudices behind and allowing our thinking to be challenged.

Envision

1. Society is beginning to recognise demographic changes and to acknowledge the increasing number of single parents—could the church respond to the needs of this significant people group by presenting singleness as a positive and acceptable option, offering hope and healing to those struggling to live amidst society's pressures? The church can give a clear lead and be a pacesetter by modelling what fulfilment is really about and providing positive role models of singleness and marriage.

2. Develop a theology of singleness that is radically different from the world view. Rediscover the biblical calling of celibacy. Teach the God-given alternative of singleness. The challenge for the church is

not to downgrade marriage but to lift singleness out of the shadows, redressing the balance and presenting a vision of what marriage and singleness can be in the plan and purposes of God. Challenge the church to take the population statistics seriously, no longer viewing single people as deviant from the norm.

3. The challenge for single men and women living in a couple-orientated society today is the challenge to be themselves, to find security, self-worth and significance in their relationship with God. The church can help single people to find their value by creating an environment in which society's pressure can be resisted and the worth and value of the single life discovered. Challenge the church to model God's provision in being the agent to offer acceptance, belonging, support, protection and release.

4. Think of the expectations that society places on children and young people. Challenge parents to consider the effect of making assumptions that growing up will result in marriage.

5. Present singleness as an opportunity: to give time, resources and gifts to God, in wholehearted devotion, and to make a significant contribution to His Kingdom. Challenge the church to see single people as a potential to be released, into ministry or into leadership where appropriate, and not to restrict them to certain roles.

6. Challenge to ensure that church structures and meetings reflect a breadth of vision in respect of single people, rather than being focused on the nuclear family. Consider the place of family-style meetings—how can they be inclusive of, and show sensitivity for, single people?

7. Challenge the church to present singleness for a season as a positive option for young people, addressing the pressure to rush into marriage. A paraphrase of Paul's writings to the Corinthian church could read:

> Consider the privilege of Christian service which is open in a special way for single people. If you postpone marriage until you feel that it will be rather late if you leave it any longer, there are tremendous opportunities for service open to you, and for some there may be the high calling of a permanently unmarried life.

The *Singularly Significant* booklet published by the Evangelical Alliance describes how in China, during the Cultural Revolution, young people were required to remain single until their late twenties with the purpose of serving the state. Would the church consider an equivalent challenge for voluntary singleness to serve God? What a resource would be unleashed! The greatest fear to be addressed would be 'What if I miss out on marriage as a result?' We need to encourage our young people to trust God and to understand that He honours every response they make to Him.

Equip and encourage

1. Challenge to care, to provide a good supportive environment in which to listen. Understand issues of identity, loneliness, sexuality, children or childlessness, bereavement and loss. Show sensitivity to pressures, to times of vulnerability and of adjustment to changing circumstances, and to responsibilities relating to home and family and future. Consider specific seminars or events designed to address particular needs and issues facing single people.

2. The church as a body emphasises the 'corporate' relationship of the church to Christ. It illustrates a dynamic expression of diversity, yet all are one body, with every member being a vital part, regardless of marital status. An emphasis on marriage and nuclear family life unwittingly invalidates singleness. There are no wasted parts in the body—the

proper working of each individual part causes the growth of the body (Eph. 4:16). A positive response from both single people and married people is important. Both need to help one another to understand attitudes and assumptions that lead to certain patterns of behaviour. Married people give advice to single people, yet sometimes single people are expected to restrict their care to other single people, or singles are expected to serve families and not the other way round.

3. Challenge the church to be a prophetic statement of God's redeemed community. Historically, a calling that includes celibacy has only been considered possible within a closeted monastic community. We need to model community *in* the world. Challenge the church to be creative in its inclusion of all singles into the family. Consider different ways of community living. Make room for extended families. Encourage singles together to create a home. Care for and befriend the elderly who live alone.

4. Encourage covenant relationships and support those seeking to be radical in their relationships. Break concepts or mindsets of our preconceived ideas about friendships. Allow a healthy expression of intimacy. Develop an understanding of Christ-centred relationships: singles and marrieds together, single people and families, single people together.

5. The church needs to be sensitive in promoting a positive approach and understanding of God's plan and purpose for our lives, which may include unfulfilled desires. The Bible does not say, 'If you desire it enough you'll get it.' We need to be careful of a prosperity gospel, but also to be positive in presenting God's will as pleasing and acceptable, for God does promise to meet every need.

6. Challenge the church leadership to teach biblical standards of morality and to face issues relating to sexuality with honesty and openness. Addressing sexuality in public meetings will facilitate discussion at a more personal level. Specific forums for safe, honest dialogue can be constructive if positively led.

Difficulties can be discussed without embarrassment or fear of condemnation among men only or women only. Married people, if included in these forums, can develop their understanding.

7. Challenge the church to support those who are determined to abstain from sexual relationships, praying for protection and for courage to resist temptation and remain pure.

8. The church's response to single people needs to include an understanding of the practical help, support and advice that single people may require.

Evangelise

1. The unchurched often perceive the church as having an irrelevant message, imposing an impossible and outdated lifestyle on its members. Explore creative and appropriate forms of evangelism that will reach out, with a relevant message of hope and acceptance, to men and women searching for security and value. The church can be the agent of healing for those who are hurting from damage in relationships.

2. In developing friendships in our neighbourhood, treat each single person as an individual of worth, regardless of marital status, sexual orientation or lifestyle. Single people are often excluded from 'partner-style' social events because they 'don't fit'. Jesus broke cultural barriers in His response to people. In contradiction to the dominant culture, to the 'social lepers' in society today, Jesus brings a powerful message of hope which is demonstrated by 'Kingdom community'.

3. Be relevant and inclusive in our evangelism, in language and culture, and sensitive to specific, often marginalised, groups, e.g. single fathers, homosexuals.

4. Demonstrate the real meaning of love to people bombarded by a distorted picture.

CHAPTER 11

OTHER QUESTIONS TO CONSIDER

If marriage is God's original plan, is singleness therefore a result of the Fall?

Genesis 1—3 makes no statement as to how relationships would develop, only how they began. God's original plan in marriage was for relationship and procreation—Adam and Eve's marriage was perfect before sin spoiled God's plan. There was no singleness before the Fall, but man destroyed the perfection of creation. In a fallen world, there is both conflict and breakdown in marriage and unfulfilment and frustration in singleness. However, Jesus came to redeem what was lost at the Fall, and His redemptive grace can transform singleness and transform marriage.

If marriage is God's intention, isn't singleness second-best?

This view is based on an interpretation of Genesis 2 that God made Eve for Adam and in so doing made the pattern for all that followed. It is important to remember that Genesis is the book of beginnings and to be careful not to base a whole theology around one section of Scripture. If singleness is second-best, why did God tell Jeremiah not to marry? Why was Paul, the great apostle, single? Most important, why did God choose to express His humanity in the perfect life of Jesus as a single person, fully man?

Why was Jesus single?

1. Jesus, the second and last Adam, came and showed

perfection in singleness to redeem the effects of the Fall. Jesus upheld God's original plan of marriage and throughout His life demonstrated how both marriage and singleness can show God's glory to a fallen world.

2. Jesus' life as a single person was also a prophetic statement of the age to come where there will be no marriage. The church is Christ's bride: He gave His life so that He could be one with her.

3. It was probably necessary for Jesus to be single to fulfil the demands of His ministry, to be undistracted in His devotion to God, to demonstrate real union with His Father and to be free to lay down His life. Consider the implications if He had married and fathered children.

Why are there so few single church leaders?
Is marriage seen as a criteria for leadership? Are single people seen as immature, unable to carry responsibility, unlikely to stay around in one place or not equipped to deal with certain aspects of leadership? Do single people not see themselves as leaders, due to perceptions or upbringing?

At the one extreme there is the Roman Catholic church which has seen virginity for priests as the means of releasing time and energies into devotion to God, and therefore requires it for priesthood (this would appear to be based on Paul's exhortation to the Corinthian church to abstain from sex in order to devote themselves to prayer). At the other extreme, churches have interpreted literally Paul's advice to Timothy that leaders should be the husband of one wife. Somewhere in the middle others would see that single people are capable of limited leadership responsibility, i.e. they would not be able to teach, pastor or counsel on issues related to marriage or children. In fact their usefulness may be restricted to other singles of the same sex. This shows incredible prejudice, since no similar restrictions are placed on married people teaching or counselling singles. Being single did certainly not restrict Jesus or Paul in their teaching on marriage, sexual ethics, etc. I do not believe the Bible says that a person's marital status affects their eligibility to lead in the church.

If single people have greater freedom and availability, should we therefore prefer to appoint single leaders?
It is important that we do not appoint leaders on the basis of their marital status, but it is healthy to see a leadership team which is reflective (but not representative) of the church population, and therefore encompassing a breadth of perspectives. We must guard against seeking to choose a 'token' single leader whom we expect to represent the entire single population!

Should the church have a separate singles' ministry?
The Bible places special emphasis on caring for widows and orphans, a reflection of God's heart for the marginalised and the isolated. Paul instructs Timothy that families and the church should show particular support for widows as they were especially vulnerable in New Testament times. Perhaps the challenge for the church today extends to the divorced and to single parents, not just in the church but in the community as well? Focusing on their needs may involve arranging activities for their children while providing opportunities for them to enjoy meeting with adults. The aim of any singles' ministry must be to release a tremendous untapped resource in our churches—to realise the potential of single people.

Is there a place for singles' groups within the church?
Groups or occasional forums for people in similar circumstances may be helpful for a season and with a specific purpose, particularly to share similar needs and provide support. All initiative and leadership must be with single people. The aim of integration in the church family must be foremost, to ensure that groups do not become exclusive or self-perpetuating, and end when the objective is met. There are times when it is helpful to have something organised where single people can

meet each other socially. However, the church is not a social club, and the best way to meet people is by getting involved in activities, home groups, etc. The church should be an environment in which real friendships are made. It is important that single people get involved in a church where God wants them to be, rather than hunt out a church where the best marriage partners are to be found!

Is there a place for advertised singles' holidays?
Organised singles' holidays for Christians can be valuable for many singles, although they often have the reputation of being dating agencies. Particularly for people within small churches, where there may be few people of similar age, interest and financial position, they can be a useful resource for meeting others, and developing friendships. I would advise caution at involvement in any secular singles' organisation/club/holiday for a single Christian on their own, as these generally have completely different standards and terms of reference.

CONCLUSION

Paul, writing to the Corinthians, described the church as a body made up of many parts. He exhorts us to treat those parts which we think of as less honourable with special honour (perhaps single people in today's culture?). 'God has combined the members of the body . . . so that there should be no division in their body, but that its parts should have equal concern for each other' (1 Cor. 12:24–25). May the church recognise those with the gift of marriage and those with the gift of singleness as of equal value. May they grow together so that any barriers between married and single are broken down as understanding of each other grows, until we attain the maturity of being all one in Christ Jesus.

The greatest challenge to the church today is to live as a radical expression of community that gives credibility to the gospel. I believe that, as we embrace a Kingdom perspective on singleness, our understanding of Christian marriage will also deepen. Our young people will grow up in, or come into, an environment that models and teaches the choice to be single and celibate, as well as the choice to be married. As older singles and divorcees also choose to accept their singleness, the church will be that prophetic statement of the redeemed 'family of God'.

To be single in the decade of the 90's requires faith to live contrary to the prevailing culture. As the church breaks some moulds and takes a positive stand, celebrating singleness and marriage in its radical message of relationship, it proclaims a prophetic statement to the nation which could turn the tide and help bring God's Kingdom to its fulfilment.

BIBLIOGRAPHY

John White, *Eros Defiled* (IVP, 1977).
Julia Duin, *Sex and the Single Christian* (Marshall Pickering, 1990).
Evangelical Alliance, *Singularly Significant* (1989).

THE WORSHIPPING CHURCH

Noel Richards

This Pioneer *Perspective* is a book written as a result of Noel's experiences as a worshipper and worship leader. He writes to help bring insight and practical help, in order that we can come to a better understanding of what it means to be a true worshipper, and of the role of worship in the life of the individual and the church.

It is often too easy to regard worship as being what we do in the corporate setting of a church meeting. Worship, though, is far greater than simply singing songs—it is about us offering our lives as a living sacrifice to our creator God.

The book challenges the church as a body to make changes where necessary. Noel suggests practical methods of blending together old and new styles of worship, wherein worship can reflect the church's vision (or lack of it!). Worship can then be prophetic or nostalgic. Are you ready to take up the vision?

Catalogue Number YB 9730   £3.99